HOOPS HEROES

by Paul Ladewski

Scholastic Inc.

New York   Toronto   London   Auckland   Sydney
Mexico City   New Delhi   Hong Kong   Buenos Aires

Photos:

Front cover (left to right): Sam Forencich; D. Clark Evans; Steve Babineau

Back cover (left to right): Garrett Ellwood; Ned Dishman; Gary Dineen

Interior: (3) Noah Graham; (5) Gary Dineen; (7, 27) Ned Dishman; (9) D. Clarke Evans; (11) Terrence Vaccaro; (13) Jacob Andrzejczak; (15) Fernando Medina; (17) Ned Dishman; (19) Sam Forencich; (21) Andrew D. Bernstein; (23) Allen Einstein; (25) Sam Forencich; (29) Melissa Majchrzak; (31) Garrett Ellwood

ISBN-13: 978-0-545-09420-7
ISBN-10: 0-545-09420-8

Copyright © 2009 by NBA Properties, Inc.

12 11 10 9 8 7 6 5 4 3   9 10/0

Designed by Cheung Tai
Printed in the U.S.A.
First printing, January 2009

BRANDON ROY

BRANDON ROY

Portland Trail Blazers guard Brandon Roy has a lot of excellent moves, but the best one of all happened off the court.

As a junior in college, Brandon played with a Washington team that included forward Bobby Jones and guard Nate Robinson — both went on to play in the NBA themselves. Considered to be one of the best in school history, the team advanced to the Sweet Sixteen of the NCAA Tournament.

Brandon could have turned pro after that, but he decided to stay in school. It was a smart move. Not only was he able to spend more time in the classroom, but he improved his game and impressed the NBA scouts at the same time.

"I really got to look back to my moments at the University of Washington during my senior year," said Brandon, who averaged 20.2 points per game in his final season. "Those moments really prepared me for where I am at today."

Today Brandon is a rising young star with a rising young team.

In the 2005–06 season, the Trail Blazers watched the playoffs on television. The team needed a talented player to build around who would also set a positive example for others. So when the Trail Blazers had a chance to acquire Brandon in a trade with the Minnesota Timberwolves on the night of the 2006 NBA Draft, they were quick to do it.

Brandon isn't the type to wow people with fancy dunks. He plays a smart game and uses his size and ball-handling ability to his advantage. At 6-foot-6, 229 pounds, he can shoot over smaller defenders and drive past bigger ones to the bucket.

Brandon can play a number of positions. Although listed as an off guard, he moves to small forward or point guard when necessary. As Trail Blazers general manager Kevin Pritchard likes to say, "Brandon is so good that he's whatever position he wants to be."

Even though Brandon sat out several games because of a heel problem in his first season, he earned T-Mobile Rookie of the Year honors. He averaged 16.8 points and 4.0 assists per game. More importantly, the Trail Blazers won 11 more games than they had the previous season.

Last season, Brandon and the Trail Blazers took another step forward. Brandon was selected to play in the All-Star Game, and the team was one of the surprises in the league.

Brandon was born on July 23, 1984, in Seattle. As a freshman at Garfield High School, he played for the junior-varsity team. He wasn't happy about it, either.

"After that year, I went to work," Brandon remembers. "I tried to develop my game so that coach couldn't say I had a weakness. The following year, I was a starter on the varsity. My goal was just to develop my game as much as possible, accept criticism and get better from it."

As someone once said, Brandon is so good that he can be whatever he wants to be.

MICHAEL REDD

MICHAEL REDD

When you see Milwaukee Bucks guard Michael Redd sink jump shot after jump shot, it's hard not to rub your eyes. The guard drains them from as far away as 30 feet from the basket.

To be an accurate outside shooter takes a lot of pride and a lot of talent. And Michael has both.

"Shooting is a lost art," says Michael, who got his nickname, Silky, because of it. "I want to be one of the artists who is remembered for a long, long time."

At 6-foot-6, Michael can shoot over smaller guards with ease. Put a taller forward on him, and the 215-pounder can rely on his strength and quickness to get to the basket.

Michael can handle the ball with either hand, but he shoots with the left one almost all the time. Because there are so few left-handers in the league, defenders don't get much practice against them. That makes Michael an even more difficult challenge.

When Michael gets on a roll, it practically takes a straightjacket to stop him.

In one memorable game against the Chicago Bulls in the 2006–07 season, Michael and Ben Gordon scored a nice, round 100 points between them. Michael finished with 52 big ones, while Ben had 48 for his team. When the smoke finally cleared, the Bulls had won the shoot-out in overtime.

Michael was "Redd" hot against the Utah Jazz in 2006–07 season. He went off for 57 points, more than any player had scored in team history. But wouldn't you know it — the Bucks lost again.

"It probably would have felt better if we had won the game." Michael admits.

Michael was born on August 24, 1979, in Columbus, Ohio. He attended Ohio State, but after his junior year, he decided to turn pro.

When the Bucks selected Michael in the 2000 NBA Draft, they got one of the best second-round picks ever. As a rookie, Michael provided instant offense off the bench. He also learned a lot from Bucks guard Ray Allen, whom he often played against in practice.

One season later, Michael was more comfortable with NBA life on and off the court. In the fourth quarter of a game against the Houston Rockets, he swished eight three-pointers, which stands as a league record.

In the 2003–04 season, Michael was a starter for the first time in his career. He averaged 21.7 points per game and was invited to the All-Star Game.

"You want to go out there and lead your team to victory," says Michael. "That's what it's all about, whether it be making plays for others or scoring or rebounding."

Michael is the son of a minister, and a devout Christian. After he signed his first contract, he bought a building for his father's church in Columbus.

Off the court, Michael likes to bowl. His favorite meal is spaghetti and meatballs. He would like to become a broadcaster one day.

His next career will have to wait awhile, though. Michael is an artist now, and there are too many beautiful rainbow jump shots left to paint.

PAUL PIERCE

PAUL PIERCE

Sometimes people are compared to others. You hear it in professional basketball all the time: This guy should play like that guy, and that guy should play like this guy.

But as Boston Celtics top scorer Paul Pierce will tell you, rather than try to be like somebody else, it's better to concentrate on what you do best.

"Once people start making comparisons to a player of the past, they want you to be that player," Paul says. "I try to go out there and create my own image, my own style, my own type of game." In 10 seasons in the league, Paul has done just that. Ever since the Celtics picked him in the first round of the 1998 NBA Draft, he has been a starter. In the 2001–02 season, Paul scored more points than any player in the league. One season later, he sank more free throws than anybody. His name appears in the Celtics record book many times.

At 6-foot-7, Paul has the strength to play forward and the athleticism to play guard. He has a deadly outside shot. Paul also can put the ball on the floor and head to the basket.

But Paul isn't only successful because of his physical skills. He considers the mental part of the game to be important, too. In his mind, Paul pictures what his opponent likes to do on the court. At the same time, he thinks about ways to attack the other guy.

"I visualize myself, the shots I'm going to get in the game, how I'm going to play defense, what we have to do to stop the other team's best player, what it's going to take out of me — the whole aspect of the game," says Paul.

Paul is known as "The Truth". Los Angeles Lakers center Shaquille O'Neal gave him the nickname in the 2000–01 season.

"I knew he could play, but I didn't know he could play like this," Shaq said at the time. "Paul Pierce is the truth."

Paul was born on October 13, 1977, in Oakland, which is located in northern California. He grew up in Inglewood, a Los Angeles suburb in the southern part of the state.

At Inglewood High School, Paul was cut from the varsity team in his freshman and sophomore years. He thought about a transfer before deciding to stay put and work hard at his game. Paul improved so much that he played with future NBA star Kevin Garnett in the All-American Game in his final year.

When Kevin and guard Ray Allen were traded to the Celtics before the start of last season, Paul was as excited as anybody on the team. For the first time in a long time, the Celtics were a serious threat to capture the Eastern Conference championship.

Paul trained hard in the summer. When the veteran showed up at training camp, he weighed 230 pounds, the lightest he had been since his college days at the University of Kansas. Then Paul, Kevin, and Ray shaved their heads to show they were on the same page.

And they were on the same page — leading the Celtics to an NBA championship. As for Paul, he won Finals MVP honors as well.

That's the truth about The Truth.

STEVE NASH

STEVE NASH

To see Steve Nash operate with the basketball in his hands, one thinks of a mouse in a maze. Steve stops and starts, changes directions, stops and starts, changes directions, then stops and starts some more. When the Phoenix Suns guard finally spots his goal, he feeds an open teammate or darts to the bucket or drains an outside shot himself.

The way Steve plays basketball is sort of like the story of his life. He knows where he wants to go — and how to get there.

"My approach has been that a player with determination and a willingness to work harder than anyone else can accomplish anything," Steve says. "It's a simple formula. I've found that it works."

Steve was born in South Africa. At a young age, his sports-minded family moved to Canada, a country known for three things — hockey, hockey, and hockey. As a kid, Steve was a puckhead like everyone else. He and his younger brother Martin also played soccer.

It wasn't until Steve was 12 years old that he began to regularly play basketball with his friends. The more he liked the game, the more he played. And the more Steve played, the better he was.

By the time Steve reached eighth grade, he could dribble with either hand and was confident enough to make a bold prediction to his mother. He told her that he would play in the NBA one day. Sure enough, in the 1996 NBA Draft, the Suns picked Steve in the first round. He was the 15th player to be selected.

It took a while for Steve to get a hang of the pro game. As a rookie, he spent a lot of time on the bench.

In 1998, he was traded to the Dallas Mavericks, and Steve began to come into his own.

"Once I figured out I could play in the NBA, I also figured I could be an All-Star," says Steve.

In 2002, Steve played in the All-Star Game for the first time. Then, along with Michael Finley and close friend Dirk Nowitzki, he led the Mavericks to the Western Conference Finals one year later.

Steve returned to the Suns after the 2003–04 season. Since then, the 6-foot-3, 178-pounder has taken his game to another level.

In the 2004–05 and 2005–06 seasons, Steve was selected Most Valuable Player in the league. He became only the third guard to capture the award in consecutive seasons. You've probably heard of the other two players — Magic Johnson and Michael Jordan.

Steve is known mostly for his abilities as a passer, ballhandler, and floor leader. In three consecutive seasons, he led the league in assists.

Because the main role of the point guard is to get his teammates involved, Steve doesn't look to shoot the ball often. Even so, he is one of the most accurate ever. Steve entered the 2007–08 season with the third-best free-throw percentage and fifth-best three-point percentage in league history.

If you're a defender, that's a problem. Get close to Steve and he can dart past you. But back off of him and he can sink the shot.

"I have gone through my ups and downs but managed to do all right," Steve says. "It's a pretty classic tale."

SUNDAY AT 6:00PM. TICK... ...OR AT SUPERSONICS.COM

TRACY McGRADY

TRACY McGRADY

Almost everybody would like to be the go-to guy on his team, but Tracy McGrady is one of the few players who has what it takes to be one.

Not only does Tracy have the talent to fill up the basket, but the Houston Rockets top gun isn't afraid to miss, either.

"Many times the game comes down to the final shot," says Tracy, a 6-foot-8 guard who has unusual size for the position. "I want to become a better clutch performer. That's what separates the really good players from the really great players."

Last season Tracy showed that he can be a really great player. At one point, T-Mac led the Rockets to 22 victories in a row! In league history, only the 1971–72 Los Angeles Lakers have won more consecutive games (33).

Not only that, but Rockets big man Yao Ming sat out a few of the games because of a foot injury. As a result, Tracy had to do more than usual. He also answered any questions about his ability to be the team leader.

"You can't take anything away from them," says Boston Celtics head coach Doc Rivers, whose team finally snapped the streak. "I don't care who plays."

In his sixth season in the league, at 23 years of age, Tracy averaged 32.1 points per game. He was the youngest player ever to accomplish the feat. T-Mac also was the top scorer the next season, when he scored 62 points in one game.

Would you believe that Tracy once scored 13 points in 35 seconds?

The explosion took place against the San Antonio Spurs in the 2004–05 season. The final points came with 1.7 seconds on the clock, when Tracy sank a three-ball for the 11th, 12th, and 13th points. The basket gave the Rockets a one-point victory.

Tracy was born on May 24, 1979, in Bartow, Florida. He attended Auburndale High School, where baseball was his favorite sport for a while. Tracy began to change his mind in his junior year, when he averaged 23.1 points and 12.2 rebounds per game.

Soon Tracy was offered a scholarship to Mount Zion Christian Academy, one of the best teams in the country. There he played all five positions and led the Mighty Warriors to a 20–1 record.

The Toronto Raptors selected Tracy in the 1997 draft. He joined Kevin Garnett, Kobe Bryant, and Jermaine O'Neal on the list of players who went from high school to the professional level.

In 2000, Tracy was dealt to the Orlando Magic and played four seasons with them. Then T-Mac headed to Houston as part of a big seven-player trade.

Now Tracy thinks it's a blast to be a Rocket.

"When you don't have to go out there and score 20 or 30 points every night, it's fun," Tracy says. "When you can pass the ball to your guys and they're making shots, it's fun."

LEBRON JAMES

LEBRON JAMES

Nobody can do more in a game than LeBron James, the Cleveland Cavaliers superstar forward. He scores, passes, rebounds, steals the ball — everything except singing the national anthem and selling cotton candy, it seems. So if any NBA player can average a triple-double in an entire season, then most experts agree that LeBron is the guy to do it.

LeBron believes it, too. In a television commercial before last season, "King James" said that to average a triple-double was one of his goals.

"There is a lot of pressure put on me, but I don't put a lot of pressure on myself," LeBron says. "I feel if I play my game, it will take care of itself."

A player is credited with a triple-double when he records double figures (10 or more) in three categories in a game: points, assists, and rebounds. The term became popular in the 1980s, when Los Angeles Lakers guard Magic Johnson would often get a bunch of points, rebounds, and assists in a game.

Because basketball has changed over the years, however, it will be difficult for LeBron or any other player to average a triple-double in one season. Teams used the fast break more often back then, and as a result, there were more points, assists, and rebounds each game. Still, in the 2006–07 season, LeBron moved closer to his target. He averaged 27.3 points, 6.7 rebounds and 6.0 assists per game.

LeBron put up numbers that were even better last season. He was selected All-Star Game Most Valuable Player and led the Cavaliers to the playoffs again. In a game against the Houston Rockets, he became the third-youngest player to reach 15 triple-doubles in his career.

Who are the other two players? Magic Johnson and Oscar Robertson.

Like Magic and Oscar, LeBron has special athletic talents that allow him to play almost anywhere on the court. At 6-foot-8, 250 pounds, he can pass like a guard, score inside and outside like a forward, and rebound like a center.

"To all the positions, I just bring the determination to win," LeBron says.

LeBron was born on December 30, 1984, in Akron, Ohio, where his mother, Gloria, raised him. He attended St. Vincent-St. Mary High School, where he was one of the best prep players in basketball history.

When the Cavaliers made him the first pick of the 2003 NBA Draft, LeBron was only 18 years old. To say the least, he has come a long way in a short time.

"I brought him up to be his own man, to make good decisions," Gloria says. "He hasn't let me down."

While LeBron has confidence in his ability, he never puts himself ahead of his team. Whatever the Cavaliers need to be successful — a basket, an assist, a rebound, or a steal — Mr. Triple-Double is ready, willing, and able to get it for them.

"I don't need too much," LeBron says. "Glamour and all that stuff don't excite me. I am just glad that I have the game of basketball in my life."

DWIGHT HOWARD

DWIGHT HOWARD

The NBA has had its share of great slam-dunk artists over the years. In the 1970s, Julius Erving threw 'em down better than anyone. In the 1980s, Michael Jordan and Dominique Wilkins did some great stuff. The torch has been passed to Kobe Bryant and Vince Carter since then. These players all stood between 6-foot-5 and 6-foot-8, and played either guard or forward. What the slam dunk didn't have was a true big man to take it to a higher level.

Then the Orlando Magic big man Dwight Howard came along.

In only four seasons in the league, Dwight has given dunkers somebody to look up to for a change. At any shape or size, the 6-foot-11, 265-pound center has to be considered one of the most creative ones in hoops history.

In the first round of the 2008 Sprite Slam Dunk Contest, Dwight threw the ball off the back of the backboard, caught it, then dunked on the other side. The judges gave him a perfect score for his performance.

Before his next attempt, Dwight put on a Superman costume, cape and all. He soared through the air from a few inches inside the free-throw line, then threw the ball through the basket. Dwight received another perfect score.

In the final round, Dwight performed two more sensational slams. On the last one, the ball was balanced on a miniature hoop placed on the backboard. Dwight raced in from the right side, snatched the ball then threw it down like a human windmill. In a fan vote, 78 percent said he was the winner of the event.

"It means a lot," Dwight says of his Slam Dunk championship. "It's really for the big men. Everybody always says big men can't jump and big men don't look good dunking. I just tried to add a little bit of my personality. With me being so tall, I knew it was going to be tough, but I just tried to play to the crowd and have fun."

But Dwight wants to be known for more than his dunks, because he can do more on a basketball court. A lot more.

Dwight takes pride in his ability to play defense and rebound the ball. Just as no NBA player had more dunks than he did the last three seasons, none grabbed more rebounds, either.

And, remember, Dwight is only 23 years old.

"The sky is the limit for that kid," says Boston Celtics star Kevin Garnett, who, like Dwight, went directly from high school to the pros. "It's almost scary."

Last season Dwight became a more complete player. He worked on his moves around the basket and averaged more than 20 points per game for the first time in his career. Dwight was also a starter in the All-Star Game.

As much as Dwight treasures his Slam Dunk title, he would like the Most Valuable Player Award even more. The reason is, the MVP often is the best player on the best team in the league.

"I want to be one of the best players in the league before I finish playing," says Dwight, who has a lot of good ball ahead of him. "I've got the talent and the heart and the right mindset to accomplish that goal. I know I can do it."

KEVIN GARNETT

KEVIN GARNETT

In life, there are followers and there are leaders — and there are those who are somewhere in between. You don't have to be around Kevin Garnett very long to know where he stands.

"I've been a leader practically my whole life," says Kevin, the Boston Celtics star forward. "I don't know what it is to follow."

As far back as high school, Kevin wanted to be the first in line. He was born on May 19, 1976, in Mauldin, South Carolina. His family moved to Chicago, where he attended Farragut Academy. Chicago has had a number of excellent high school players over the years, and many experts consider Kevin to be the best of them all.

The Minnesota Timberwolves selected Kevin at the fifth pick in the 1995 NBA Draft. He was the first to advance from high school to the pros in 20 years.

Since then, Kevin has grown in size and maturity. The boy in him has never gone away, though. Few athletes enjoy the game more than Kevin, who plays like a 32-year-old man and acts like a 16-year-old kid.

On the court, Kevin is very active. In his career, he has averaged nearly 21 points, 12 rebounds, and five assists per game. At 6-foot-11, 253 pounds, Kevin has a long, athletic body that allows him to play almost any position if necessary.

On the bench, Kevin is enthusiastic as well. He yells and claps his hands to encourage teammates and recognize good plays.

"I go crazy trying to energize people because that's what I am," says Kevin, who also is a big soccer fan. "I'm a battery. If you're down, you can plug into me and get charged up."

Kevin is charged up a lot these days.

In the 2003–04 season, Kevin carried the Timberwolves to the conference finals for the first time in their history. As hard as they tried, though, they couldn't get over the hump. After the 2006–07 season, Kevin was traded to the Celtics in return for five players and two draft picks. No team ever gave up more bodies for one player in NBA history.

In Boston, Kevin joined guard Ray Allen and forward Paul Pierce. All of sudden, the Celtics had three All-Stars in their lineup. A league championship became their goal.

"I would love to do something that would make everybody I care about proud that Kevin Garnett was around," Kevin says.

In 12 seasons with the Timberwolves, Kevin accomplished a lot. He was chosen league Most Valuable Player and All-Star Game MVP one time each. Eleven times he was an All-Star selection. Twice he led the league in rebounds. Once he led the league in points. He was the first player ever to average at least 20 points, 10 rebounds, and five assists in six consecutive seasons.

"Satisfied? No, I'm not satisfied," Kevin says. "There's a lot I want to get done in the NBA."

Whether or not Kevin achieves his goals, one thing about him will remain the same. He'll always love the game. He'll always wear a smile when he plays it.

"It's all about having fun, playing hard and fair, and not hurting anybody," Kevin will tell you. "Feel good about what you're doing and how you're doing it."

In 2008, Kevin definitely had fun — in fact he had a *lot* of fun — winning a title with the Celtics.

MANU GINÓBILI

MANU GINÓBILI

One of the best things to happen to the NBA in the 1990s was the increased number of foreign players. And few players have done more than Argentinean-born Manu Ginobili, the ball of fire who has helped lead the San Antonio Spurs to three league championships.

"Without playing in Europe, I never would have made it here," says Manu, the only player ever to be a part of Euroleague, Olympic, and NBA championship teams.

When the Spurs chose him in the second round of the 1999 draft, they got one of the biggest steals ever.

Hard to believe, but 56 players were drafted ahead of him!

"Manu was just a young skinny guy who looked like a winner," remembers Gregg Popovich, the Spurs head coach. "We didn't know he was going to be as good as he is."

Rather than sign with the Spurs immediately, Manu returned to Italy, where his team was one of the best around. Twice he was selected Most Valuable Player of the Euroleague, which is similar to the NBA overseas.

In 2002, Manu played his first NBA game. At first, the rookie struggled to find himself, partly because of injuries and partly because of the new style of play. But as the season got older, Manu and his team got better. The Spurs went on to capture the NBA crown, as Manu played a key role off the bench.

In the 2004–05 season, his third in the league, Manu started every game he played in, was invited to the All-Star Game, and raised his performance in the playoffs, averaging 20.8 points and 5.8 rebounds per game. He finished second to teammate Tim Duncan in the Most Valuable Player vote as the Spurs won it all again.

The next season Manu was bothered by injuries. But in the 2006–07 season, he bounced back to help lead the Spurs to another championship. When the team needed more energy off the bench, Manu was the one to provide it. He averaged 16.5 points per game, more than he had ever scored before in his career.

"I just try to do what I do best and contribute to my team," says Manu, whose name is pronounced MAN-oo Jih-NOH-buh-lee.

Off the court, Manu is just an average guy. He likes to surf the Internet, listen to music, and watch movies. He also can speak three languages well.

On the court, Manu is more effective than smooth. Manu plays such an aggressive, physical style that it seems like he is on the floor more than he is on his feet sometimes.

"I don't play like this because I want to look pretty," he says. "I think people can really see I love the game."

Manu is a good outside shooter, but at 6-foot-4, 205 pounds, he isn't afraid to take the ball to the bucket, either. His ability to draw fouls close to the basket is unusual for his size.

The fact that Manu is left-handed also makes him difficult to cover. His moves surprise many defenders who rarely have to defend against smart, shifty southpaws such as himself.

"I think people can really see I love the game," Manu says. And anyone who has ever watched him play knows he does.

BARON DAVIS

BARON DAVIS

Patience and hard work can lead to success. How do we know this to be true? Just look at Baron Davis, for one.

Mostly because of injuries, Baron never realized his potential in nearly six seasons with the Charlotte and New Orleans Hornets. It wasn't until three years after Baron was traded to the Golden State Warriors that he became recognized as one of the best point guards in the league.

In the 2007 playoffs, Baron was lights out. In round one, he led the Warriors past the Dallas Mavericks in one of the greatest upsets in NBA history.

The Utah Jazz eliminated the Warriors in the second round, but not before Baron pulled off one of the most memorable dunks of the season. He threw down a one-hand slam over forward Andrei Kirilenko, who had a six-inch height advantage. Overall, Baron averaged 25.3 points, 6.5 assists, and 4.5 rebounds per game in the playoffs.

"It's just motivation for me to know that a lot of people have me low on the totem pole right now," Baron says. "I'm just trying to prove them wrong."

Baron has a good sense of humor, likes to talk, and is good with words. He is popular among his fans and teammates.

Opponents don't like Baron quite as much, though, because he does so many things well on the court. What makes Baron a special player is his strength, reflexes, and ability to handle the ball. At 6-foot-3 and 215 pounds, he can either outquick or outmuscle an opponent to the bucket for layups. Baron also is a very good rebounder for his size.

Even more impressive is how Baron has been able to overcome a difficult childhood.

"As good a player as Baron is, he's an even better person. He has overcome a lot of hardships to get where he is now," Warriors head coach Don Nelson says.

Born on April 13, 1979, in Los Angeles, Baron and his sister Lisa were raised by their grandparents in a tough part of town. His grandmother Madea encouraged him to play basketball at a young age. He was so good that he received a hoops scholarship to attend Crossroads School, a private school in Santa Monica, California. Then, between his sophomore and junior years, Baron grew five inches! All of a sudden, he stood 6-foot-3 and could dunk a basketball.

Several colleges expressed an interest in Baron before he chose UCLA. He averaged 13.6 points and 4.4 assists per game in two seasons, then decided to turn pro.

The Charlotte Hornets selected Baron as the third pick of the 1999 draft. He led his team to the playoffs five times, and played in the 2002 and 2004 All-Star Games. In February, 2005, Baron was traded to the Warriors, and his return to California brought out the best in him.

"I definitely want to finish as the best point guard in the NBA," Baron says. "If I'm the best point guard in the NBA, it means that we're winning and we're a playoff team."

CHAUNCEY BILLUPS

Did you ever feel like a square peg in a round hole? You're not alone. For years, Chauncey Billups felt the same way.

Early in his career, Chauncey moved from team to team to team, but none was right for him. Now that the point guard has found a home with the Detroit Pistons, there is nowhere else he would rather be.

"In the NBA, it's about patience," Chauncey will tell you.

Born on September 25, 1976, in Denver, Chauncey went to college at the University of Colorado and was a star player there. In the 1997 NBA Draft, the Boston Celtics selected him at the third pick. Like many rookies, Chauncey started slowly. He was traded to the Toronto Raptors midway through the season.

Next, Chauncey moved to Denver, but he didn't stay there long. He was traded to Orlando a few weeks later. Because of an injury, though, he never played a game in a Magic uniform.

"This is a tough, tough life when things aren't going your way," Chauncey says.

As frustrated as he was at the time, Chauncey never quit on himself. After the 2000–01 season, the Minnesota Timberwolves signed him to come off the bench. When a starter was injured, Chauncey stepped in and played well.

A few weeks later, Chauncey headed to Detroit, where he finally found a home. The Pistons needed someone like Chauncey to be their floor leader. And Chauncey was a fan of Pistons general manager Joe Dumars, who was an All-Star guard once himself. In fact, Chauncey wore uniform 4 in college because it was the one that Joe wore in the pros.

It took six teams and six years, but Chauncey finally found a place where he fit. Since then, he has developed into one of the game's best point guards.

"I wasn't always considered one of the best, so I want to stay there as long as I can," said Chauncey, who played in the last three All-Star Games. "That's what pushes me every single time I'm on the court."

At 6-foot-3, 202 pounds, Chauncey doesn't have a noticeable weakness in his game. On offense, he is a threat to score anywhere within 25 feet of the basket. As a ballhandler, he makes few mistakes. On defense, Chauncey sticks to his man like Velcro. As one of the team captains, he is a fearless leader.

Chauncey usually is at his best late in the game. He is called Mr. Big Shot because of his ability to come up big when the score is close.

Chauncey was never better than in the 2004 NBA Finals, which saw the Pistons capture the league championship. He averaged 21 points and 5.2 assists per game and was selected Most Valuable Player of the series.

Chauncey could have packed up and headed to another team after the 2006–07 season. Instead, he agreed to a deal that could keep him with the Pistons for five more seasons.

After all, when you're at the right address on the right street, why not kick back and stay awhile?

KOBE BRYANT

KOBE BRYANT

When fans talk about the best player in the NBA today, a bunch of names are sure to be mentioned. But anyone who believes that Los Angeles Lakers guard Kobe Bryant is The Man can make a pretty good case.

Start with three league championships. Add two league scoring titles. And 10 All-Star Game appearances. And two All-Star Game Most Valuable Player Awards. And nine All-NBA selections. And eight All-Defensive selections. And his Slam Dunk Contest championship. And his 2008 MVP award . . .

"I'll do whatever it takes to win games, whether it's sitting on a bench waving a towel, handing a cup of water to a teammate, or hitting the game-winning shot," says Kobe, who at 30 years old still has plenty of big shots left in him.

Kobe Bean Bryant was born on Aug. 23, 1978, in Philadelphia. His parents named him after a type of beef called Kobe, which they saw on a menu in Japan. His middle name is short for Jellybean, which was his father Joe's nickname while he played in the NBA for eight seasons.

"My parents are my backbone," Kobe said. "They still are. They're the only group that will support you if you score zero points or you score 40."

When Kobe was six years old, Joe decided to play basketball in Italy and moved his family overseas. Kobe learned to speak Italian, and played soccer and basketball there.

In 1991, the Bryants moved back to the Philadelphia area, where Kobe was a star at Lower Merion High School. Kobe considered a scholarship offer to attend Duke, but he decided to head to the NBA instead. Only 17 years old at the time, he was the first guard in history to make the jump from high school to the pros.

In the 1996 draft, the Charlotte Hornets drafted Kobe at the 13th pick in round one. Before Kobe played a game for them, however, he was traded to the Lakers. The deal was one of the best ever made.

Like all young players, it took a while for Kobe to feel comfortable. But when he got his game together, he and center Shaquille O'Neal led the Lakers to three league championships in a row.

Kobe was so gifted and so athletic that people started to compare him with Chicago Bulls great Michael Jordan, his favorite player as a kid. But as much as Kobe likes Mike, "I don't want to be the next Michael Jordan," he says. "I only want to be Kobe Bryant."

In 2006, Kobe did something that Michael never did in his sensational career. In a game against the Toronto Raptors, he scored 81 points! The only player to score more points in one game was Wilt Chamberlain, who exploded for 100 points in the 1961–62 season. When you consider that Wilt was 7-foot-1 and Kobe is 6-foot-6, the performance is even more impressive.

"There's been a lot of talk of me being a one-man show, but that's simply not the case," Kobe says. "We win games when I score 40 points and we've won when I score 10."

CHRIS BOSH

CHRIS BOSH

At 24 years old, Chris Bosh is the main man of the Toronto Raptors, and one of the brightest young stars in professional basketball. But Chris shows that athletes can do more than run fast, move quick, and jump high. They can also be well-rounded people with smarts and personalities at the same time.

Known as CB4, which are his initials and uniform number, Chris knows the value of education. He was born in Dallas and attended Lincoln High School there. Not only did Chris lead his team to the state title, but he also was a member of the National Honor Society. Chris speaks to youth groups about how important it is to read, something he likes to do often.

Chris can be a funny guy, too. On an Internet video last season, he pretended to be a character named Chris W. Bosh, a used-car salesman who begged fans for their All-Star Game votes.

Indeed, Chris may be a man of many interests, but playing basketball is what he does best.

Born on March 24, 1984, Chris was a star at Georgia Tech. As a freshman, he averaged 15.6 points, 9.0 rebounds, and 2.2 blocked shots per game.

Chris wanted to complete his degree in graphic design and computer imaging, but his game was so good that he couldn't pass up the chance to play professional basketball. So Chris left Georgia Tech after one season, but not before he promised his mother that he would return to college one day.

The Raptors selected Chris at the No.4 pick of the 2003 NBA Draft. It took him only four seasons to become a team leader in points, free throws, rebounds, and blocked shots.

At 6-foot-10, 230 pounds, Chris is similar in size and style to Kevin Garnett, the Boston Celtics star. His jump shot is deadly in the 15- to 18-foot range. He can drive to the bucket, and he is an excellent free-throw shooter as well.

In the 2006–07 season, Chris started to come into his own. He averaged 22.6 points, 10.7 rebounds, and 2.5 assists per game, some pretty impressive numbers to say the least. More important, as one of the most valuable players in the league, Chris led the baby Raptors to their first Atlantic Division title. Midway through the season, fans began to chant "M-V-P! M-V-P! M-V-P!" when he did something special at the Air Canada Centre.

As much as the Raptors like to have his 20-plus points and 10-plus rebounds each night, they need Chris to be a leader every bit as much. As the one who sets the example for the rest of the team, Chris makes sure to play as hard on offense as he does on defense every game.

"I try to be a presence on the boards and on the defensive end," Chris says. "I just try to be where I am supposed to be. Just that alone helps the defense out a lot."

Oh, and about that All-Star thing? Last season Chris was a member of the Eastern squad for the third consecutive season.

Ladies and gentlemen, Chris W. Bosh appreciates your support.

CARLOS BOOZER

CARLOS BOOZER

For 18 seasons, Karl Malone and John Stockton were one of the best combinations in professional basketball. Karl played power forward, John played point guard, and the Utah Jazz teammates made beautiful music together. Many believe there will never be another pair quite like them on the same team.

Well, don't look now, but Carlos Boozer and Deron Williams are pretty good copycats already. With the help of Deron, the Jazz point guard, Carlos ranks as one of the best power forwards in the game. Some consider the 27-year-old to be a younger Mailman, as Karl was called all those years.

"My favorite memory of Karl is not from on the court," Carlos remembers. "It was the first time I met him and shook his hand. I was just blown away. Even though we have different games, I really respect Karl as a person and as a player."

While Carlos can score in several different ways, his sweet spot is 8-to-12 feet from the basket. There the 6-foot-9, 266-pounder can maneuver for a dunk or hook shot with either hand. His turn-around jump shot also is very accurate and difficult to challenge.

Born on Nov. 20, 1981, in West Germany, Carlos grew up in Juneau, Alaska. He attended Juneau-Douglas High School and led the Crimson Bears to two state championships in a row.

Wherever Carlos plays, his team seems to be successful. Carlos played college ball at Duke and helped them capture the 2001 national championship while he was there.

In 2002, the Cleveland Cavaliers drafted Carlos in the second round of the NBA Draft. Carlos showed a lot of potential early in his career — he averaged 15.5 points and 11.4 rebounds per game in his second season — but the team let him become a free agent.

The Jazz signed Carlos, and they're mighty glad they did. In his first season with the Jazz, Carlos averaged 17.8 points and 9.0 rebounds every game. The Jazz quickly discovered how valuable he was to the team. Carlos suffered a hamstring injury that forced him to sit out the last part of the season. Without their best inside player, the Jazz failed to qualify for the playoffs.

At the start of the 2005–06 season, Carlos hurt his hamstring again. He sat out the first half of the season. When Carlos returned to action in late February, he came off bench. After so many months on the sidelines, though, he was excited to play anywhere.

"I felt like the first day of school or something," says Carlos, who played in the last two All-Star Games. "My heart was beating a little faster, my anticipation was building up."

One month later, Carlos was a starter again. Since then, he has taken his game to an even higher level.

As good as Carlos was in the 2006–07 regular season — he averaged 20.9 points and 11.7 rebounds per game — the Jazz man was even better in the playoffs. He averaged 23.5 points and 12.2 rebounds, and led his team to the Western Conference finals.

Hey, the Mailman isn't the only power forward who delivers in Salt Lake City, you know.

CARMELO ANTHONY

P rofessional basketball may be serious business, but it's supposed to be fun more than anything else. To judge by the expression on his face, does anyone enjoy himself more than Carmelo Anthony, the Denver Nuggets star foward?

On game nights, Melo flashes a smile that can light up a room. "You've got to have fun on the court," he says. And he's no different off the court, either. After a few minutes together, even strangers feel like they have known him for years. His friendly personality attracts people like a magnet.

"I smile all the time, even when I'm in a bad mood," Melo says. "I always try to keep a smile on my face."

Don't let the frown turned upside down fool you, though. When Melo is on the court, he is very serious about the game.

What Carmelo does best is put the ball in the basket. Because Melo makes a high percentage of his shots, he doesn't have to take many to get his points. At 6-foot-8, he can operate close to the basket. He also has a sweet midrange jump shot that is difficult to block. Melo can even step back and hoist a three-pointer once in a while. And he likes to rebound, too.

Even with more than one defender close to him, Carmelo can be effective. He is a team guy who will give up the ball for the Nuggets to be successful.

Last season Carmelo experienced the best of his five seasons in the league. Not only was he selected to start for the Western Conference All-Star team for the first time, he received more votes than anyone at his position. During the season, in a victory against the Washington Wizards, he scored more points in one game — 49 — than he'd ever scored before.

Carmelo was born on May 29, 1984, in New York City. When he was eight years old, his family moved to Baltimore. In high school, Melo grew five inches one summer, and a few months later, he was named Baltimore Catholic League Player of the Year. Before his senior year, Melo transferred to powerhouse Oak Hill Academy in Virginia, where he was selected to the All-America team.

Melo spent only one year in college, but what a year it was! He led Syracuse to its first national basketball championship. He was named the Most Outstanding Player of the NCAA Tournament after he scored 33 and 20 points in the final two games.

In the 2003 NBA Draft, the Nuggets were in search of a young talent they could build around, so they chose Melo at the No. 3 pick. As a rookie, he averaged 21.0 points per game. Better yet, one year after they had been the worst team in the league, the Melo-led Nuggets advanced to the playoffs.

At 24, Melo has leadership qualities that are uncommon for his age. In 2006, he was selected co-captain of the United States Men's Senior National Team. If the United States captures the gold medal in the 2008 Summer Olympics in China, expect Melo to have a smile wider than Denver when he returns home.